AND IT CAME TO LAUGHS

Cover art by David Burnett

Cover design copyrighted 2005 by Covenant Communications, Inc.

Published by Covenant Communications, Inc.
American Fork, Utah

Copyright © 2005 by David Burnett
All rights reserved. No part of this book may be reproduced in any format or in any medium without the written permission of the publisher, Covenant Communications, Inc., P.O. Box 416, American Fork, UT 84003. This work is not an official publication of The Church of Jesus Christ of Latter-day Saints. The views expressed within this work are the sole responsibility of the author and do not necessarily reflect the position of The Church of Jesus Christ of Latter-day Saints, Covenant Communications, Inc., or any other entity.

This is a work of fiction. The characters, names, incidents, places, and dialogue are products of the author's imagination, and are not to be construed as real.

Printed in Canada
First Printing: August 2005

11 10 09 08 07 06 05   10 9 8 7 6 5 4 3 2 1

ISBN 1-59156-941-9

". . . so for the last year of my mission I served as a Canine Distraction Specialist. If you had a door you couldn't get to, I was your man."

"Hold it right there, Sister Snavely! Now, turn around slowly, walk back to the D.I. trailer, and remove Brother Snavely."

"... so this concludes our home teaching message for April. Now, before we leave, Wally and I would like to say how much we enjoy being your home teachers!"

For the rest of his life, Melvin Smullen would never forget to wear a tie to church after having to wear one from his bishop's special collection.

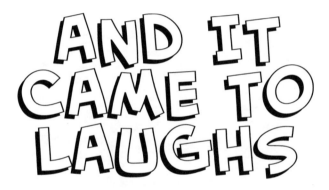

by David Burnett

"The steroid rumors were totally unfounded!"

Every Sunday, for ten long years, Brother Jaworski, a restless child, and some zombie named Bob mindlessly wandered the church hallways.

"Well, well, Mr. Studebaker! You sicced Old Blue on us, and we converted him. Who's next, Mr. Studebaker? The cat? The chicken? Heck, we'll even take on the iguana!"

"I can't believe that you seriously think anyone would want to shake that hand of yours after what happened last Sunday!"

Due to the nonstandard hours required by his crime-fighting career, Bishop Farley often had to conduct meetings in his uniform.

"Laman! Lemuel! Say hello to our new home teachers!"

"... and after the ward choir, the Relief Society will present a bedpan decoration demonstration. And then after that, the Scouts would like to publicly apologize for that unfortunate camping incident."

An even sharper trader than his dad, Johnny Lingo Jr. forever marks Tallulah as the "One-Chicken Woman."

"Greetings! I, Elder Higgins, Honorary King of the Monokuwowkus, have returned!"

"You forgot to take out the garbage—again!"

**Place: Newel K. Whitney store
Time: July 4, 1836
Event: Near riot erupts during first Blue-Lantern Special**

"You know what you need here, Myrtice? A Real Man! One who will take you in his strong arms and make you feel safe and secure!"

"Oh, don't be ridiculous! What's a few thousand miles in a cardboard box to a grandmother who misses her favorite grandson?"

"Perhaps we should discuss what 'Gathering the Righteous' actually means, Elder."

"We'll now hear from Elder Farnsworth about his exciting mission amongst head-shrinking natives."

"Oh, Harold! Not the entire food storage again!"

"... so one day when Frank was really tired and stressed out from his ward duties, I said, 'Frank, what's the most relaxing thing you can think of to do?'"

"Look, Brother Herbert—you're 104 years old and you've outlived three wives. Don't you think it's time to give it a rest?"

"She promised at the airport to wait forever, and then this happens. Hopefully, his second day here at the MTC goes better than the first."

Brother Mooney's "Scratch and Sniff" missionary ties were always a big hit on Family Home Evening nights.

"Oh look, Brother Griffin. Todd's here to make his annual tithing payment . . . in pennies."

A typical ward "Matchmaking Committee."

"Spare me the theatrics, Brother Johnson.
You're not getting out of this calling."

"Just think of all the years we told our kids, 'Sit up straight like the Browns! Be reverent like the Browns! Pay attention like the Browns!' And now it turns out the Browns are just a bunch of mannequins."

"Pardon me, ma'am, but could I trouble you to unplug your bug zapper for just a moment?"

Stanley Snodgrass: Official member of the Missionary Hall of Fame since 1958.

"All right, you guys! Who brought the dragster?"

"A little lighter on the hands next time, brethren."

Defying all odds, Elder Elder, Elder Berry, Elder Bishop, and Elder Apostle show up at the same mission on the same day.

"Oh look, children! Your father's finally been released from the bishopric!"

"Elder Livingstone, I presume!"

". . . Jones here is a bank president, Burk owns an oil company, I'm a state senator, and . . . uh . . . what exactly was it that you said you do, Elder Chuckles?"

"Warn the mission presidency? Are you kidding? These guys are the mission presidency!"

"Here's your mail, Sister Barnes, and . . . uh . . . do you think your son would mind if we borrowed his bike for a couple of days?"

"Sorry about the plane ticket, Elder, but look at the bright side . . . you'll be delivered right to your very own front door!"

"Don't be scared, children . . . This is your father, and he's been on the high council for the last five years."

"Well, Brother Burns. Jimmy and I have had a nice little chat, and he has agreed to stop his silly pranks and be the best scout he can be!"

In contrast to his cousin Johnny Lingo, Delbert Lingo was known as the most incompetent trader in the islands.

"... and the most disturbing item is this computerized age-enhanced photograph of your so-called boyfriend! Perhaps you would like to reconsider my proposal, Shelia."

Following a freak accident in his laboratory, ward membership clerk Mervin Tweetle often had trouble obtaining a correct attendance count.

Caught up in the excitement of her first year at college, Thelma quickly forgets her father's stern warnings against wearing rose-colored glasses.

Pioneer Monster Wagon Event

"Enjoy your peach fuzz while it lasts, Elder."

"Burt's still as handsome as the day we married!"

1849: First missionaries arrive in Transylvania, traveling without hearse or crypt.

"Watch out for that bowl in the back of the fridge, Elder. Rumor has it that it's been there since the eighties."

"OK! OK! I admit it! My mother did everything for me! I can't feed myself, I can't dress myself, I can't even make my bed or brush my teeth! Mommy!!!"

Morbonics

"Elders, according to our records, your area was shut down over sixty years ago. Do either of you recall ever receiving release forms that looked like this?"

"This is what we unofficially call the 'RM Freeze.' First weekend back they try dancing with a female and then just sort of freeze up."

"... and that story reminds me of another exciting high council experience!"

David vs. Goliath: The untold story

"Will that be one or two cows today, Mrs. Carlson?"

"Do you suppose he's just taking a power nap?"

"Oh great! We're infested with Sunbeams again!"

"Sorry folks, but we're going to have to choose another winner. Brother Mortonberg thought he was in the food line."

"But President, these are my lucky tracting shoes!"

"Since you were too busy to do your home teaching on Earth, we figured we'd load you up here."

Throughout his entire education, the Brother of Jared never completed a single exam.

"The bishop says it's 'Shoulder to the Wheel' until things pick up around here."

"Well, hello there! Welcome to the Nursery!"

"Martha, the bishop here requests that we make a generous offering."

"Looks like Lonnie's adjusted really well since coming home from his mission."

"How does 'Singles Representative for One Hundred and Over' strike you?"

"We'll now be privileged to hear from Elder Dewberry, former president of the Lilliput North Mission."

Next to her education, the Smacker XR-5000 was the best investment Doreen ever made.

"Good thing we had that Jack Mormon handy!"

"Sounds like someone finally tried Sister Hagerman's squid casserole."

"Well, whadaya know . . . the jawbone of an ass!
You gotta permit for this, buddy?"

"Coool! This toothpaste tube looks almost exactly like the diaper rash tube!"

"I don't care what you're the leader of! I'm still your mother, and I say you're going to Sunday School class!"

Tired of the continuous harassment over his lack of hair, Elisha purchases a toupee.

Next season's Survivor: Ken Jennings, Donny Osmond, Steve Young, and Johnny Whitaker battle to the last man on Antelope Island.

"Okay, boys, now the elephants. Shem, pitch 'em some hay. Japheth, give 'em plenty of water. Ham, you . . . uh . . . well shoot! You know what you need to do."

After forty years of regrets and denial, former Primary dropout Henry Heblinger recites the thirteenth Article of Faith and receives his long-coveted bandelo from his former Primary president.

Forced to land at Roswell, Elijah's chariot becomes UFO #1327098-B and is never seen again.

"Dear Brethren . . . stop. Work momentarily delayed on Manti Temple . . . stop. Need time to resolve small problem . . . stop."

After countless false leads and dead ends, Primary President Edith Zinkleworth finally cracks the infamous CTR Tattoo case.

**Although a dedicated elders quorum president,
Chuck McFarland was often guilty of micromanagement.**

DAVID E. BURNETT was born and raised in North Florida. He served a two-year mission in the Utah Salt Lake City Mission, attended Ricks College, and graduated with a BS in manufacturing engineering technology from Weber State University. He is employed with the Intel Corporation in Colorado Springs, Colorado. In addition to cartooning, he also enjoys music and songwriting and has played with several local bands over the years. He and his wife, Cindy, have four children and live east of Colorado Springs.